VOLUME 5

Miss Brenda's

BEDTIME STORIES

This book is lovingly presented to

_____

By: _____

On this special occasion

_____

Date: _____

VOLUME 5

Miss Brenda's
BEDTIME STORIES

BRENDA WALSH

Based on
**True Character-Building Stories
for the Whole Family!**

3ABN BOOKS

Three Angels Broadcasting Network
P.O. Box 220, West Frankfort, Illinois
www.3ABN.org

Pacific Press® Publishing Association
Nampa, Idaho
Oshawa, Ontario, Canada
www.pacificpress.com

Design/Layout: Chrystique Neibauer "CQ" I cqgraphicdesign.com
Cover Photography: David B. Sherwin
Project Coordinator: Mellisa Hoffman I finaleditservices.com
All images used under license from Shutterstock.com, unless otherwise noted.
Other inside photos, unless otherwise noted, have been provided by the author.

The author assumes full responsibility for the accuracy of all facts and quotations as cited in this book.

Additional copies of this book are available from two locations:

Adventist Book Centers®: Call toll-free 1-800-765-6955 or visit http://www.adventistbookcenter.com.

3ABN: Call (618) 627-4651 or visit http://www.store.3abn.org.

3ABN Books is dedicated to bringing you the best in published materials consistent with the mission of Three Angels Broadcasting Network. Our goal is to uplift Jesus Christ through books, audio, and video materials by our family of 3ABN presenters. Our in-depth Bible study guides, devotionals, biographies, and lifestyle materials promote whole person health and the mending of broken people. For more information, call 618-627-4651 or visit 3ABN's Web site: www.3ABN.org.

Scripture quotations marked NIV are from the HOLY BIBLE, NEW INTERNATIONAL VERSION®. Copyright © 1973, 1978, 1984 by International Bible Society. Used by permission of Zondervan Publishing House. All rights reserved.

Scriptures quoted from NKJV are from The New King James Version, copyright © 1979, 1980, 1982, Thomas Nelson, Inc., Publishers.

Scripture quotations marked NLT are taken from the Holy Bible, New Living Translation, copyright © 1996, 2004, 2007. Used by permission by Tyndale House Publishers, Inc., Wheaton, Illinois 60189. All rights reserved.

Scripture quotations marked KJV are from the King James Version of the Bible.

Library of Congress Cataloging-in-Publication Data:

Walsh, Brenda, 1953-
Miss Brenda's bedtime stories : true character building stories for the whole family! / Brenda Walsh.
    p. cm.
ISBN 13: 978-0-8163-2515-3 (hard cover)
ISBN 10: 0-8163-2515-4 (hard cover)
1. Christian children—Religious life—Anecdotes. 2. Families—Religious life—Anecdotes.
I. Title. II. Title: Bedtime stories.
BV4571.3.W35 2011
249—dc22

                                                                    2011007590

11 12 13 14 15 • 5 4 3 2 1

The Micheff Family

Not a day goes by that I don't stop and thank the Lord for my precious family! In a world where families are falling apart, I realize that it is only God's amazing love and the prayers of my parents, that binds us so closely together. When I walk back over memory lane and remember the sacrifices my parents made just to keep us connected with Jesus, my heart overflows with gratitude for them! Dad and Mom provided a *Christ-centered* home, and faithfully led our family in morning and evening worship. They also encouraged my brothers and sisters and me to have our own private devotions and to depend on Jesus for everything.

Dad and Mom didn't have the money for church school, but God honored their faith by opening the bank of heaven and providing the means for all five of their children to receive a Christian education. Before leaving the house each day, we would all kneel in a circle, hold hands, and pray for God to keep us close to Him and for us to be a witness to all we met. Dad ended every prayer with "Lord, may our family be gathered together in heaven when You come in those clouds of glory, and may there not be one lost!" That prayer has never left me and has now become not only my prayer for my family, but for all of God's precious people. I long to see the work here on earth finished so that we can all live eternally with Jesus! May the promise in Acts 3:25 be fulfilled in each one of us . . . *And in your seed all the families of the earth shall be blessed.*

My precious family, I love you with all my heart and I'm dedicating volume five of *Miss Brenda's Bedtime Stories* first and foremost to our precious heavenly Father, and then to each one of you. I love you with all my heart and it is truly my deepest desire to spend eternity with you in heaven . . . without one missing!

ACKNOWLEDGMENTS

With Special Thanks

Dr. Kay Kuzma

I want to thank Dr. Kay Kuzma for all her hours and hours spent editing *Miss Brenda's Bedtime Stories*. She is one of the most generous, kind, and talented people I know and these stories would not have been the same without her! I admire and respect her professionalism, creative writing skills, and her loving service for others. Her love for our Lord and Savior shines through in all she does. She has blessed my life in so many ways and I thank God for the gift of her friendship.

Brenda Walsh

Author Appreciation

I want to personally thank each of these best-selling authors and friends for their generous contribution of stories. It is truly an honor and privilege to include them in this book. Each author was personally selected to be a part of *Miss Brenda's Bedtime Stories* because of their creative and professional writing style, incredible talent, and love for Jesus! To each of them, I extend my sincere and heartfelt thanks!

John Bradshaw

Karen Collum

Mark Finley

Karen Holford

Kay Kuzma

John Lomacang

Charles Mills

Kay D. Rizzo

Kimberley Tagert-Paul

Danny Shelton

Jerry D. Thomas

Don Vollmer

ACKNOWLEDGMENTS

With Heartfelt Thanks To . . .

MY STORY AND PHOTO TEAM: *Battle Creek Academy* for opening your doors for the cover photo shoot. *Mellisa Hoffman* for your project coordination, organizational skills, being the "spelling champ," tenacity to *getting the job done*, and your loyalty and friendship! *Hannah and Lance Hoffman* for your patience during all the long hours your mom spent working on the book project. *Dr. Buddy and Tina Houghtaling* for organizing and planning the cover photo shoot, and all the years you dedicated your life to *Kids' Time!* *Chrystique Neibauer* for the incredible layout and graphic design of the entire project, for extra long hours, patience, and being a friend I can count on! *Dave Sherwin* for volunteering your time to photograph each cover.

MY MINISTRY SUPPORT TEAM: *Carole Derry-Bretsch* for your love, support, constant Christian witness, and, most of all, for being my lifelong friend! *Peg O'Brien Bernhardt* for always being there for me, listening, believing in me, and for your love and friendship! *Marie Macri* for being a precious friend—always there for me. I love you dearly! *Rita Showers* for a lifetime of memories, friendship, and the best neighbor a girl could have! *Nancy Sterling* for being my mentor, looking out for my best interests, and for your loving friendship!

MY FAMILY: My precious husband, *Tim Walsh,* for never complaining about the time I spent working on this project, for your constant support, help, and patience, but most of all, for your unconditional love you give me every day! *Rebecca Lynn and Linda Kay* for your love and support and allowing me to share your stories. My parents, *James and Bernice Micheff,* for your prayers, letting my team take over your house, for endless hours finding photos, and for all those great meals! To my *sisters, brothers, grandsons, aunts, uncles, nieces, and nephews* for your patience and loving understanding concerning the many hours I spent working on this project, even though you would have preferred I was spending time with you! I am so very grateful for my precious family and love you with all my heart!

Those who shared their stories with me:

Dianne Affolter	Trinity Murray
Hannah Hoffman	Ron Reese
Bonnie Humpal	Andy Rissing
Nancy McDowell	Nancy & Jenna Sterling

The Freak Wave

I t was an exciting time for Seth because he, his brother, Aiden, and their dad were going to attend their church's Thanksgiving campout. They would be camping on the beach for four days listening to stories, singing, eating good food, and having fun with their friends.

This was a first for Seth. His mom was not interested in religious things, so he seldom went to church. But now that he was living with his dad, church was a very important part of their lives.

"What will we do at the campout?" Seth asked.

"I think we'll do a lot of praising the Lord for the things He has done for us this year. Thanksgiving is a wonderful holiday. And since so many of us aren't able to travel to the mainland where the rest of our families live, we're going to celebrate with our next best family— our church family."

Seth was so excited about the campout that he could hardly wait. Every morning as he got ready for

school, he would ask his dad, "When do we leave for the campout?"

"Soon," his dad would say. But to Seth, it seemed like *soon* would never come. At last, the day finally arrived.

Seth and Aiden had a hard time deciding which part of the church campout they liked best: camping out in their tent, the yummy food, or the daily afternoon hiking adventures.

On Thanksgiving morning, Seth and Aiden joined the others for worship. They especially loved singing songs about Jesus. Then came the most delicious Thanksgiving dinner. Seth had never seen so much food in his whole life. People came from all over the Hawaiian island of Kauai bringing stir fry, ginger and sesame seasoned noodles, sticky rice, purple sweet potatoes cooked in coconut milk, papaya, bread fruit, taro, and so many yummy desserts!

After lunch, Seth's friend, Malachi, suggested, "Let's go hiking on the Anini Beach trail."

Everyone thought that was a great idea, so Seth, Aiden, and their dad joined the group of hikers as they took off on the rocky trail that skirted the ocean front.

Seth was having the time of his life. He was jumping from one lava rock to another and then racing over the sand stretches to the next rock outcropping.

"Wow!" Dad commented to his friend who was hiking with him. "I can't believe the ocean is so calm back at Anini Beach and here it looks like a raging sea."

Just then, Seth ran past his dad and jumped down to the sand. "Seth, slow down. You've got to be careful on these rocks. They could be slippery. You could trip and I could never rescue you if you fell into the ocean here." Seth paid no attention. In fact, he acted as if he hadn't heard a word his dad had said.

A little farther up the trail, they met a couple of hikers who were camping on the beach not far away. They mentioned that the waves in this area could be treacherous. "We had to move our camp farther away from the ocean the other night because the waves were so high." Then, pointing to Seth, they added, "And watch that kid, especially in the sandy places between the rocks. The tide's coming in and if he doesn't stay on the trail through the bushes, he could get washed into the ocean."

With that warning ringing in his ears, Dad caught up to Seth and had a serious talk with him about the dangers of the ocean—specifically telling him that when he hit the patches of sand to stay on the alternate trail up by the bushes.

"OK, Dad." Seth acted as if he understood the message his dad was trying to get across to him. But a few minutes later, he ran ahead and, without thinking or even glancing toward the ocean, jumped down to the sand and ran to catch up with Malachi, who was on the other side of the sandy patch. As he jumped, Dad yelled, "Seth, stay on the trail by the bushes!" but the pound of the surf was too loud for Seth to hear—and the words too late.

Suddenly, a freak wave reared out of the ocean bed, crashed on the rocks, and pounded the sand with a *thud*. The wave was so high it hit Seth in the chest, knocked him over, and began to drag him away. All Seth had time to do was scream, "Help!" at the top of his lungs. Malachi had seen the wave coming and was already in the process of running toward Seth. Instantaneously, he grabbed Seth's arm and yanked him to safety. Even one second later would have been too late as

Seth almost certainly would have been sucked into the deep churning water.

As the group hiked back to Anini Beach, Seth thought about his prayer at worship that morning. *I prayed for God's protection and even though I didn't listen and pay attention like I should have, God still saved my life. He must love me an awful lot!* ■

*My son, pay attention to my wisdom;
lend your ear to my understanding.*
—Proverbs 5:1, NKJV

Rita to the Rescue

"Stop! STOP!" yelled Rita as her family was driving down a country road in Tennessee.

"What's wrong?" Dad asked as he applied the brakes. *Screeeeeech!*

"There's a turtle crossing the road!"

"Rita, how do you think the turtle is going to get to the other side of the road if it doesn't cross it?" Dad teased.

"But I don't want it to get run over," Rita said as she unsnapped her seat belt and jumped out of the car.

"Be careful. It could be a snapping turtle," her mother warned.

"It's OK, it's just a box turtle . . . and from the hump on its shell, its light orange eyes, and . . ." Rita picked up the turtle and turned it over, "And the flat shell underneath means this one's a female. I think I'll call her Myrtle."

She started to put the turtle on the side of the road and then realized

that since Myrtle didn't know how dangerous the road could be, she might try to cross it again. "Can I take Myrtle home? She'd be safe in the lower pasture near the pond."

Rita was always rescuing animals. Some of her rescues included a motherless baby raccoon, an injured possum that the dogs got, and her favorite—Tripod, the adorable gray kitten that somehow had lost a leg before it came limping down the road in front of her house.

Then came the day her folks were asked to be missionaries, teaching at a Nigerian mission school. Rita found good homes for her rescued animals and was thrilled about living deep in the jungles of Africa with its new sights, smells, and exciting animals.

The family hadn't been in Nigeria very long before Rita had adopted a stray yellow cat that was wandering around their compound. She named him Leo the Lionhearted. She also felt sorry for a feisty monkey who was kept chained next to a tree. The owners were trying to tame him, but it seemed impossible. The monkey had probably been abused as a baby and had a bad habit of biting and scratching anyone who got close. When she brought up the subject of adopting him, her parents said, "Absolutely not!" Rita knew no amount of begging would change their minds, so she didn't ask again.

Then one day, Rita was watching her dad fix the front porch step when two African men in native dress came up the road. They stopped and spoke to Dad in broken English. One was carrying a very small African antelope called a *duiker* (die-ker) who had a broken leg.

"Ten *naira,*" the man said as he held out the duiker to Dad.

Dad shook his head, said, "No," and returned to fixing the step.

Then the other man stepped forward and in broken English said,

"Mama duiker killed. Baby needs home. Too little for chop-chop." Rita knew that "chop-chop" was the African word for food and she started to get worried.

Dad once again said, "No!" He pointed to the leg that was hanging limply to the side. "It has a broken leg."

The African holding the duiker said, "You fix!"

One glance at the skinny little baby with big dark eyes and a soft beige coat and Rita's heart melted. "Dad, please buy the duiker. If you don't, it will die."

Dad knew what a tender heart his daughter had toward animals, especially if they were hurt. He stood up and began to bargain with the African. "Five *naira.*"

"Eight *naira,*" the African countered.

Finally Dad reached into his pocket and counted out six *naira* and handed it to the African. Then with a big smile on his face, the African man placed the duiker on the ground in front of Rita.

She leaned over, put her cheek down on the duiker's soft back, and announced, "I'm going to call her Darcy."

By this time, Mom had joined the group of curious people who had gathered to watch the bargaining. "What are we going to feed Darcy?" Mom asked. They tried giving her all the normal things that duikers eat, such as leaves, shoots, seeds, fruit, buds, and bark. But she refused them all.

Rita sat down on the step and began to pray. *Dear Jesus, please help Darcy eat something or she's going to die.* Suddenly, she felt Darcy nudge her leg. Mom took one look and exclaimed, "She's trying to nurse."

Quickly they filled a baby bottle with warm milk and, sure enough, the baby duiker began to drink the milk.

Now they had to figure out how to splint the duiker's broken leg so it would heal right. "We don't have any plaster for a cast," Dad said. "Let's think . . . what else could we use?"

Someone suggested bamboo. "Great idea," said Dad. "We've got lots of bamboo on campus. We could slip Darcy's leg inside the hollow part. The bamboo will keep her leg straight until it heals." So as Mom watched the little duiker, Rita and her dad went to find just the right size of bamboo. Then they cut the bamboo just a little longer than the leg, drilled holes in the top, and taped it into place. They threaded the rope through the holes and stretched it around the back of the duiker to hold the splint in place. It worked perfectly. When Darcy got up to walk, she dragged the splint behind instead of stepping on it, thereby keeping the weight off her broken leg so it would heal. A month later, her leg was as good as new.

By this time, Dad had built a pen for Darcy next to the house and soon the duiker was jumping around and diving under the bushes, just as if she were living in the wild. But while most duikers were afraid

of cats—because they often ended up as chop-chop for leopards and lions— Leo became Darcy's best friend. They slept together, playfully boxed each other's noses and ears, and then Leo would jump on Darcy's back. Around and around Darcy would go with Leo skillfully balancing on her back. If

Leo fell off, he would jump right back up again. The kids on campus loved to watch and laugh as the two unlikely friends performed. It was like a circus act.

Before Rita knew it, two years had gone by and her family was planning where they were going on furlough. They would be gone for three months visiting family and friends in the United States and touring some interesting countries in between. It was time to find homes for Rita's pets. Leo was easy—all the kids on campus wanted him. But Darcy needed a special home, so they made arrangements for her to live with some other duikers at the Ibadon Zoo.

As Rita was sitting next to her parents on the long flight to the United States, thinking about her life in Africa, she commented, "Thanks for all the pets you let me have. You're the best parents. I'm probably the only girl in the world that's had a pet duiker!"

"Well, you've always been our 'Rita-to-the-rescue'! God's given you a special love for all His animals."

"You're right, Dad. But when I think of all the fun times I've had with my pets, I think they've really done more for me."

As Dad put his arm around Rita and gave her a big hug, she looked up and said, "I sure hope Darcy's having fun at the zoo!" ∎

> *"If you then, being evil, know how to give good gifts to your children, how much more will your Father who is in heaven give good things to those who ask Him!"*
> —Matthew 7:11, NKJV

Finders Keepers

Jake trudged up the steep hill towards his house. It had been a long day at school and his backpack was digging into his shoulders. The hill was one of the steepest in town and every morning he hurried down the path to the bus stop and every afternoon he slowly climbed back up.

Just a few steps from the top of the hill, Jake kicked a stone and sent it skipping for quite a distance. It landed under some bushes. That's when he saw it. Slightly off the main path . . . was a man's wallet.

Jake's heart was racing as he reached down and picked it up. When he opened the wallet hoping to find out who it might belong to, he gasped. There was more money inside than Jake had ever seen in his whole life. The bills lined up like pages of a book. He was so excited, his hands began to shake as he pulled out the one hundred dollar bills and started counting. *One, two, three . . . thirty-nine, forty!* Jake did the

math. *Wow!* he thought. *Four thousand dollars in cash!* Jake could hardly believe his eyes.

Jake flipped his thumb across the stack of bills, quickly placed them back in the wallet, and started off towards home. He was nervous carrying around that much money. The sooner he got home, the better. *I can't wait to talk to Mom. She'll know what to do.*

To get to his house on Quarry Road, Jake had to walk past Hudson's Ice Cream Shop. Jake was so hot the sweat trickled down between his shoulder blades. *A sundae sure would taste good right about now.* He could almost feel the cold, delicious ice cream melt in his mouth. *I wish I had brought some money with me.*

Jake stopped suddenly as if he had run into a brick wall and grabbed the back pocket of his jeans. *Wait a minute. I do have money. In fact, more money than I've ever seen in my whole life!*

He shifted his weight from one foot to the other. *A sundae doesn't really cost that much. There's four thousand dollars in that wallet. Surely the owner wouldn't miss the cost of one measly sundae.* Jake imagined himself pulling out one of the crisp one hundred dollar bills and handing it over to the shop owner. He could see Mr. Hudson's bushy eyebrows jump up in surprise. Jake normally paid for sundaes in coins, so he would have to come up with some story of why he had such a big bill. Maybe he could say it was his birthday money from his grandfather.

Jake shook his head. *No, I can't. This isn't even my money and I certainly can't lie about where I got it. Sure, a sundae would be great, but the sweetness would turn sour in my belly if I used stolen money to buy it.* He set off for home at a jog.

Bursting through the front door, Jake couldn't wait to show his mom what he had found, but was only greeted by their cat, Mollie. A note was waiting for him on the kitchen table: *Dear Jake, Got called in to work the afternoon shift. Won't be home until after six tonight. Dinner's in the fridge. Love you, Mom.*

Jake collapsed in a chair at the kitchen table and held his head in his hands. After a silent prayer, he knew what he needed to do. He opened the wallet and found a library card with the name *Jackson Holmes* on it. A quick phone call to the library was all it took. The librarian said she would contact Mr. Holmes and pass on Jake's message.

That evening, just after Mom got home, there was a knock at the front door. Jake opened it and Mom came right behind him, curious as to who was there. The gentleman on the porch said, "Hi, I'm Mike Johnson. My friend would like to talk to you," pointing to a man sitting in a wheelchair at the bottom of the porch steps.

The man extended his hand. "Jake, is it? I'm Jackson Holmes. Am I ever glad to see you."

Jake smiled as he walked down the steps. "Pleased to meet you, Mr. Holmes." He held out the wallet. "I believe this belongs to you."

Mr. Holmes let out a long, slow whistle. "Well, well, well." He opened the wallet and flicked his thumb across the bills. "Some people would've thought they'd won the lottery when they stumbled across this. I thank God that you found my wallet, Jake. I've been praying about it all day." Mr. Holmes maneuvered his wheelchair a little. "You see, Mr. Johnson was taking me for my morning walk in my wheelchair and somehow the wallet fell out of my pocket. I didn't even notice it was gone until I got home. We retraced our path right away, but never did find it." He looked up at Jake. "Would you like to know what this money is for, son?"

"Sure," Jake nodded his head. "I was wondering why someone would carry around that much money."

"It's to pay my rent. I'm about to move into a new wheelchair-friendly house down on Sussex Street and they require two months' worth of rent before they'll hand me the keys. I've got until eight o'clock tonight to get it to them." Mr. Holmes' eyes filled up with tears.

Jake shuddered. *If only Mr. Holmes knew how close I had come to taking some of that money for myself,* he thought. He was thankful there wasn't a fudge sundae digesting in his stomach. Even the thought of it made him feel sick. "It's all there, Mr. Holmes. You can count it if you'd like."

Mr. Holmes waved his hand in the air. "Don't need to, son." He winked at Jake. "I trust you." He laughed a big belly laugh and looked at his watch. "Now, I'd better high-tail it down to that real estate office before they give my house to someone else. I've been on a long waiting list for a long time!" He shook hands with Jake and his mom once more. "I'm sorry I can't give you a reward, son. I really do need every cent of this."

Jake smiled. "That's OK," he said. "I don't need a reward. Just seeing the smile on your face is enough for me!"

Mom gently squeezed Jake's shoulders. "And doing the right thing is the best reward of all, isn't it, Jake?"

"That's right, Mom. You can't put a price on a clear conscience." ■

> *"You shall not steal, nor deal falsely,*
> *nor lie to one another."*
> —Leviticus 19:11, NKJV

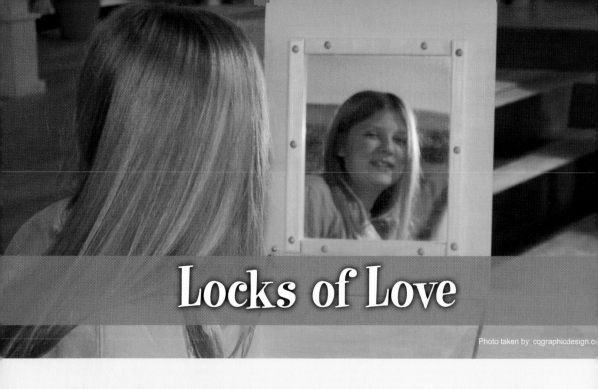

Locks of Love

"**M**om, how do you like my hair best? Up like this with a clip or pulled back in a ponytail?" Hannah asked as she swished her hair first one way then another, seeking her mom's approval.

Mom laughed. "Hannah, you have gorgeous hair—no matter how it's styled. I even like you in pigtails!"

"Pigtails? I would never wear pigtails! They're old fashioned and besides, I'm not a little girl anymore."

"It's nice that your hair is long enough so you can do almost anything with it—and it looks great. But even if you didn't have a hair on your head, I'd still think you were beautiful."

"Really?" asked Hannah laughing. "I'm just glad I have hair!"

"That's a good point. Kids lose their hair for many reasons, but God said that it's what's on the inside that is really important. I'm glad you have beautiful hair—but I also want you to have a beautiful heart!"

deep breath, looked around one last time to make sure no one was watching, grabbed the watch closest to her, and shoved it into the pocket of her jeans.

"Good girl," said Carole. "Now let's go."

Annie could feel the adrenaline racing through her veins, her heart pumping loud and fast. She followed the giggling girls as they hurried down the aisle and headed for the door, bumping into one another in their rush. They walked past the registers where everyone was paying for their purchases. The watch was burning a hole in Annie's pocket and she kept touching it, not quite believing what she had done. But the girls were right; she hadn't gotten caught and the door was only a few steps away.

Hurrying out into the center of the mall, the girls huddled together laughing and chattering about their thrilling adventure. They were so relieved at not getting caught, they didn't even notice the three store security guards surround them. All of a sudden, Annie felt a firm grip on her arm and she jumped trembling with fear. "Girls, you'll need to come with us," said a man in a deep commanding voice.

Annie had never been so scared in all her life. Customers stared as the security guards marched them right through the middle of the store to the offices at the back. It was as though everyone knew what they had done. Everyone! Annie's face was red with embarrassment and she began to cry. She wished she had never taken that watch. It wasn't like she needed it. Annie couldn't believe how foolish she had been.

Inside the security office, it got worse. The manager of the store, Mr.

Allen, spoke harshly to the girls and demanded that they return the stolen goods. Annie quickly removed the watch from her pocket and handed it to one of the security guards.

"I'm so sorry," she whimpered.

Jayne took the hat from her head and tossed it on the desk. "Here, I didn't realize it was on my head. I was just trying it on." The security guard rolled his eyes in disbelief.

Then the other girls laid down their stolen items beside the hat. Mr. Allen asked if the girls had anything they wanted to say. Annie sobbed, "I'm so sorry, really, I am."

All of sudden, her new friends weren't so friendly. "It was Annie's idea," said Jayne, not daring to even glance in Annie's direction.

"Yeah," said Melinda. "We wanted to pay, but Annie wouldn't let us."

"She said we couldn't be friends with her unless we stole something," said Carole.

Annie couldn't believe her ears. That wasn't what happened at all! "No!" said Annie. "That's not true. They're lying! I didn't want to steal anything . . ." but then her sobs smothered her words.

"I'm not interested in whose idea it was," said Mr. Allen. "As far as I'm concerned, you're all guilty." The manager sighed and lowered his voice a little. "Girls, what you did was really foolish. I'm sure you know what you did was wrong. I've decided to let you go with a warning. But if I ever catch you shoplifting in my store again, I'm calling the police and pressing charges. Do you understand?"

Carole, Jayne, and Melinda walked away quickly without even giving Annie a second glance. She could hear them giggling and laughing as they went. Then she heard one of them say, "Wow, that was a close call!"

"Mr. Allen," said Annie swallowing hard, "I'm really sorry. I've never stolen a thing in my life. I know what I did was wrong and even more importantly, I broke one of God's commandments. I want to ask you for forgiveness and I'm going to ask Jesus to forgive me too. I've learned my lesson."

"You seem like a good girl that just made a wrong choice. Let's forget this ever happened, OK?" Mr. Allen smiled kindly and reached out to shake her hand. As Annie turned to leave, he added, "Before you go, can I make a suggestion? I think you might need to find some new friends."

"Oh, they're not *my* friends, Mr. Allen. I found out today . . . they never were. I'm not choosing *phony friends* ever again!" ■

Do not be misled:
"Bad company corrupts good character."
— 1 Corinthians 15:33, NIV

Better Than Disney

Dad stopped the car on the muddy lane and turned off the engine. "Well, here we are! This is it! Our lovely little home for the next few days!"

Through the misty rain, Josh and Jenny looked at the dreary gray stone house and then at each other. "Not exactly Disney World, is it?" Josh whispered to Jenny. They both felt gloomy and bored. Their vacation in Scotland didn't look like it would be fun at all.

"Come on! Let's go inside and explore!" Mom tried to sound excited, but she was tired from the overnight flight and the long drive up and down the hills to the Scottish Highlands.

Grandpa had been born in this village, but it had been many years since he had seen his homeland. He had paid for the entire family to fly to Scotland and experience the special place where he had grown up.

The next morning, Grandma made real Scottish oatmeal porridge

for breakfast. Josh put honey and cinnamon on his, but Grandpa ate porridge the Scottish way, with salt and butter.

"Who's going to come on a walk with me to the village?" asked Grandpa. Josh and Jenny were quiet. It didn't sound like a fun place. Josh wanted to play a new game on Dad's laptop and Jenny had a book to read. "Och, come on! I have so many things to show you," said Grandpa. He spoke using Scottish words such as "och" instead of "oh," "loch" instead of "lake," "burn" instead of "stream," and "bairn" instead of "child."

"OK, I'll come, Grandpa!" said Josh.

"I guess I'll come too," Jenny said, putting down her book.

The village was a mile or so across the fields and Grandpa took them on a path alongside the stream. They passed a stone cottage with chickens scratching around outside. A lady was hanging her laundry on a line in the garden. "Why, if it's not Bessie MacBayne!" exclaimed Grandpa.

She looked puzzled for a few moments. "And if it isn't Jock MacDuff! Lovely to see you just now. And these bairns must be your grandchildren, I've no doubt! Redheaded just like you! Must be forty years since you went to America! Could you use a few eggs for your supper?" She hurried inside and found a carton of eggs. "Just laid this morning! Come by if you need some more!"

"Well, thank you so much!" said Grandpa. "I'm sure we will!"

"That was kind," said Jenny. "She hardly knows us!"

As they walked down the lane a farmer came by on his tractor. He waved to them. "Hi ya!" he said. "How's you?"

"Och, not too bad," said Grandpa. "It's a lovely morning after the rain we had yesterday, it is . . . are you a Murray?" Josh wondered what a "murray" was. Maybe it was a Scottish word for a farmer. Scottish people used all kinds of funny words he had never heard before.

"Och, yes! I'm Donald Murray! How did you know?"

"Went to school with your pa and you look just like him!"

"Well, would you be wanting a lift to the village? I'm taking some hay to the low field. You can ride in the trailer."

They climbed in next to a big bale of hay and rode down the twisting lane together. It was bumpy and fun. Josh and Jenny held on to the sides of the trailer and giggled so much that Jenny got the hiccups!

"Wow! That was almost as fun as a Disney ride!" said Josh.

In the village, Grandpa bumped into an old friend who was just coming out of the post office. "Why, it's Donald Wallace, is it not?" exclaimed Grandpa.

"And it's Jock MacDuff, is it not?" said Mr. Wallace. "And these must be your wee grandbairns!" He smiled at Josh and Jenny. "Are you young-uns having a good time up here in the glens?" He spoke very Scottish and Josh could hardly understand him.

"Well, you know," smiled Grandpa, "they're from Florida, and it's hardly Disney World out here, it is!"

Mr. Wallace chuckled. "Well, have they ever been inside a real Scottish castle?"

"Not one like yours!" said Grandpa. Jenny looked at Josh. *Grandpa has friends who live in castles? I wondered if Mr. Wallace is a prince or something.* Even Josh looked interested when the castle was mentioned.

"Well, I'm on my way there just now, if you've got nothing else to be doing. You can hop in the back!" Mr. Wallace had an ordinary blue car.

Jenny was disappointed. She hoped he might have a carriage and horses or something much more royal.

"Is Mr. Wallace a prince?" whispered Jenny to Grandpa when they arrived at the castle.

Grandpa just laughed. "No, he just looks after it. The castle belongs to a rich Japanese businessman, but he only comes here once or twice a year."

The castle was amazing! It had towers and turrets and spiral staircases. It had a cellar and a roof terrace and large halls, and even a secret passageway between the walls, hidden behind an old cupboard. Jenny walked down the large swirling staircase and pretended she was a princess floating down to a party. Josh looked over the battlements around the roof and pretended he was a guard, protecting the king.

Mrs. Wallace, who did all the cooking for the castle, served them freshly baked Scottish shortbread, and they sat and drank raspberry juice at the long table in the kitchen. Mr. Wallace took out his flute and Mrs. Wallace sang a pretty Gaelic song in words that Josh and Jenny didn't understand at all.

When it was time to go home, Mr. Wallace drove them back to the village to pick up food for lunch. Grandpa forgot that he only had American money in his pocket. But the lady in the shop said, "Nevermind, now! Just take the food and pay me tomorrow!" *Wow,* thought Josh, *people really trust each other here! They wouldn't say that at home!*

Dad was birdwatching in the garden when they got home. Josh and Jenny ran to tell him all about their adventures.

"Dad, this place is amazing!" said Josh. "Everyone knows Grandpa even though he hasn't lived here for years!"

"And everyone was so kind to us because they loved Grandpa!" said Jenny.

"And we rode on a tractor, and visited a castle, and ate shortbread, and we even got some eggs!"

"Sounds as if you had fun!" said Dad. "Even if it's not exactly Disney World!"

"Oh, Dad!" said Jenny, "I think this is better than Disney!"

"Even better than Disney? Your most favorite place in the whole world?"

"Oh yes!" Then Jenny was thoughtful. "Everyone loved us because they knew our grandpa. And everyone was so kind and trusting and friendly and . . . and . . . and just so nice!"

"You know what I think," said Josh. "I think this village is just like heaven. And now that I've been here, I want to go to heaven even more!" ■

I am not saying this because I am in need, for I have learned to be content whatever the circumstances.
—Philippians 4:11, NIV

"Oh, Dad, are you saying that I can keep Prince?" Shannon questioned hesitantly.

"What do you think, sweetheart?" Dad asked his wife.

"Prince seems to be fitting into our family just fine. It's OK with me if we adopt him."

Jacob added, "Prince needs a family . . . and we need a cat. I think it's a perfect fit."

With that, Shannon rushed over to her dad and gave him the biggest, tightest hug in the world. And then she threw her arms around her mom. "Thank you! Thank you!" she exclaimed. "I'll take good care of Prince, I promise."

"Me too," Jacob added.

"Now that we have that settled," Dad said. "Does anyone have anything they want to thank Jesus for?"

Photo taken by: Melissa Bradshaw

"I do!" Shannon waved her hand in the air. "I want to thank Jesus for Prince. When Dad didn't think it was the right time and place for me to have a cat, I began praying every day that if it was Jesus' will, He would work it out so I could have a cat. And He did! We didn't even have to go find one at the animal shelter or in the newspaper. Jesus brought Prince to us, and he isn't a homeless Prince anymore!" ■

He who did not spare His own Son,
but delivered Him up for us all, how shall He
not with Him also freely give us all things?
—Romans 8:32, NKJV

Fireworks Surprise

"**D**ad, please let me fix it. I know how," Johnny pleaded.

"I'm not sure that's a good idea," Dad explained. "You're pretty young to be fixing electrical things such as broken lamps."

"But it's just the cord that's broken. How hard can it be to splice it back together?" Johnny questioned.

Dad was hesitant. But Johnny wouldn't take no for an answer. "Come on, give me a chance. I've watched you fix broken cords before. I know exactly what to do!" Johnny stood up straight and puffed out his chest. "Please, Dad, give me a chance to prove to you that I know what I'm doing. After all, you said yourself that you're too busy to fix it now."

"I know you've watched me fix electrical cords before, but were you really watching closely? Or did you just kind of look now and then when you were curious about what I was doing?"

Without saying another word, Dad got out of the car, opened the trunk, and removed Mandy's suitcase. He placed it beside the car and then opened the car door for Mandy to get out. But Mandy didn't move! She just sat there as still as could be.

"Mandy, come on. It's time to get out. Honey, I really can't wait any longer. You're not going to find a better house than this."

At that, Mandy began to cry. "Oh Dad, I'm so sorry. I don't want a new family," she sobbed. "I don't want to live anywhere else. Really I don't. I love you and Mom and Melanie and Macie. I don't want to change families! Please, can I come home?"

"Are you sure that's what you want?" Dad looked seriously at Mandy. "You know, if you come home, you would have to do your share of the chores, obey the rules, and help your sisters when they need it. We don't have a fancy house, a swimming pool, or money to buy all the things you said you wanted."

"Oh, Dad, I don't need any of those things! I just need my real family! Please let me come home. I promise I'll never complain again!" By this time, Mandy was crying so hard her whole body shook with sobs.

Dad gently lifted her out of the car and into his arms. "Honey, of course you can come home! Our family wouldn't be the same without you! Mom and I love you very much. Let's go home and tell her and your sisters that you have decided to stay with your real family."

With that, Mandy got back in the car. Dad put her suitcase in the trunk and they drove home. When they arrived, Mandy threw herself in her mom's arms and held on tight. "Oh, Mom, please forgive me. I don't want another family. I don't want another mom and dad. You're the best mom ever and I don't want to live anywhere else."

At the sound of Mandy's voice, Melanie and Macie jumped out of their

Photo taken by: Brenda Walsh

beds and came running, smothering Mandy with hugs. "Oh Mandy, we're so glad you came home." Melanie reached over and gave Mandy a kiss. "Jesus answered our prayers."

"Yeah," said Macie. "We were praying and praying that you would come back!"

That night as Mandy knelt beside her bed, she said a special prayer of her own. *Dear Jesus, please forgive me for being so selfish and thank You so much for giving me the most wonderful family in the whole world!* ■

Lazy hands make a man poor,
but diligent hands bring wealth.
—Proverbs 10:4, NIV

So that's exactly what Dex did. The next time he looked back, Payne was gone.

As he walked home that night, Dex thought about the third part of his plan to deal with Payne. "What you really want," his dad had said, "is to turn Payne into a friend. And the Bible teaches us that the best way to do that is to treat people with kindness." Dex shook his head. *Please, dear Jesus, help me find a way to do something nice for Payne.*

Later that week, the teacher reminded the class about a special study session. "Those of you who are having trouble in English need to stay and study for tomorrow's test." Dex headed for the door. He always got good grades in English. But he noticed Payne slump into a desk at the back of the room. He thought for a second, then walked back into the classroom, smiled a friendly smile, and sat down beside Payne.

Payne glared at him. "What are you doing here? I thought all you 'A' students went home."

Dex opened his book. "Not today. I need to study for our test tomorrow."

"You? Study? I thought you were supposed to know it all," Payne said sarcastically.

"No way," Dex answered. "I have to study for every test too."

"Then why don't I ever see you here after school?"

Dex smiled. "I usually study at home. My dad's a writer and he helps me. He always wants me to get good grades in English. But he's busy today, so I thought I would stay and study here."

Payne looked at him, but didn't say anything.

Dex tried smiling again. "What does your dad do?"

Payne shrugged. "He's a mechanic. He was going to be a professional basketball player, but he hurt his knee."

"Wow," Dex said, "no wonder you're so good at basketball. When we finish studying English, will you teach me some of your basketball moves?"

Payne nodded and almost smiled. "I could do that," he said. "You need to learn some things."

Dex hid his smile behind his English book. Payne wasn't his friend yet, but he might be before long. *I can't wait to tell Dad—the plan is working!* ■

> *"Do not seek revenge or bear a grudge against one of your people, but love your neighbor as yourself."*
> —Leviticus 19:18, NIV

It made sense to Shawn, but for some reason, he was mad at his dad for allowing this to happen, even though he knew it wasn't really his fault. How he wished he were back in his old neighborhood where there were paved streets for bike riding, swimming pools in backyards, and basketball hoops.

Summer flew by quickly and before Shawn knew it, Beth and Darren had left for school. Now Shawn didn't have anyone to talk to or play with. Because they lived so far out in the country, he was going to be home-schooled, so it was going to be tough meeting kids his age, let alone making new friends.

Soon the days grew shorter and colder. One morning, Shawn saw his breath when he woke up. *"Brrrr,"* he grabbed his jacket and put it on over his pajamas. "Hey, why is it so cold in this house?" he complained.

"Probably out of propane," his dad responded.

The old house had a propane heater and a large five hundred gallon tank. Unfortunately, the Haskells were so low on funds that they weren't able to order more fuel. The minimum amount the propane company would deliver would cost more than Dad could afford.

"I think we have enough money to pay for a twenty-five gallon tank," Dad said as he left for town. "I'll just have to keep getting a refill until we can afford a delivery."

Shawn dished up some hash browns and pancakes his mom had made on her electric skillet. Without propane, the gas stove wouldn't work either. A short time later, he heard Dad return with the heavy tank. He looked out his attic window and watched his father roll it off

the back of the truck and maneuver it over to the platform where he could attach it to the propane line going into the house.

"How long do you think that will keep us warm?" Shawn called down to him.

"Oh, maybe a couple of weeks," his father replied. "Then I'll have to get some more."

All winter, because they couldn't afford to have propane delivered, Dad would take the tank to town and trade it for a full one, then wrestle it back onto the platform next to the house.

Then one day, Shawn's dad had an accident at work.

He hurt his back and wrenched his knee. He could barely walk. Unfortunately, that afternoon he needed to get another propane tank.

Shawn heard his parents discussing what he should do. "But, honey," he heard his mom say, "you shouldn't be walking on that knee. You need crutches. And I'm worried that you'll hurt your back even more."

"But if I don't go, it will be really cold in the house. I wouldn't want you to get sick!"

As Shawn watched his father limp out toward the platform to get the empty tank, his conscience started hurting. He felt guilty for not helping. Suddenly, he remembered a Bible text he had learned the year before: "I will maintain my righteousness and never let go of it; my conscience will not reproach me as long as I live" (Job 27:6, NIV).

Not waiting another moment, he grabbed his jacket and ran toward the truck. "Hey, Dad, let me do that!" he yelled.

After loading the tank into the truck, Shawn rode with Dad to town. It didn't take long to fill it up and as the attendant helped him push and shove the full tank back into the truck, Shawn asked, taking a moment to catch his breath, "How much does this thing weigh anyway?"

"Oh, a couple hundred pounds," the attendant replied, shutting the tailgate.

When they arrived home, Shawn helped his dad maneuver the heavy tank off of the truck bed and onto the platform, while his dad showed him how to attach it to the line going into the house. "Hey, thanks for your help, son. With a hurt back and a bum knee, I doubt if I could have done it by myself."

Shawn wondered why he had never offered to help his dad before. He was ashamed of himself. He was strong and able to help, and he did benefit from the heat the propane produced, but he never once thought to say Thank you for what his dad did for him, nor did it occur to him that he should offer to help. *How could I have been so selfish?*

"Dad, I've been really foolish. I blamed you for moving us out here to this miserable old house, but I know it wasn't your fault. It's meant a lot of extra work for you—especially trying to keep the house heated. Thanks for all the trouble you've gone to for Mom and me. I know you love us and are trying hard to take good care of us. I'm so sorry for the way I've been acting."

"I love you, son. I wish I could afford a better house for our family, but for whatever reason, I feel like God is just testing our faith right now. It means a lot to me to have your support." Dad reached out and put his arm around Shawn. Then he smiled and gave him a wink. " I had a feeling you'd come around."

A few minutes later, Dad smiled as he overheard Shawn say, "Hey, Mom, what can I do to help you with supper?" ∎

Serve wholeheartedly, as if you were serving the Lord, not men.
—Ephesians 6:7, NIV

Jenna's Joy

Jenna stared at the calendar. So far, eleven days had been marked off of the November page. That left only six more days until her birthday. Jenna sighed. *Six more days seems like forever. Six more days to wait until . . .*

It had started months ago when Jenna was celebrating Mallory's birthday. Mallory's aunt Bess had sent a special package in the mail. Opening the box, the girls squealed with delight as they pulled out a new doll that looked a lot like Mallory. The girls had played with the doll all afternoon. It had come with accessories like a carrier, a stroller, and even a small highchair. Before the afternoon was over, Jenna knew what she wanted for her next birthday. It would be so much fun playing with her own look-alike doll, especially on the long drives to her grandparents' home.

So, when Jenna's mom asked what she wanted for her birthday, the doll was the only thing Jenna mentioned.

I learned a lot today . . . and not just about fishing."

"You're welcome, Jason. Never be too proud to ask for help. That's the way you learn," Dad added.

"And it helps to have a great teacher. I guess that's what Dads are for," said Michael.

Photo taken by: David Coffin

"Hey Dad, can we stop by and show Captain Burt the fish I caught?" Jason asked.

"Yeah, Dad, can we? I can't wait to see the look on his face," Michael added.

"I don't know why not," Dad smiled. "I'm sure he'll be excited to see Jason's big catch!" ■

My son, hear the instruction of your father.
—Proverbs 1:8, NKJV

Kasi Fights Back

"**B**aba, what are you doing home so early? And why are you so sad?" Kasi asked her dad as he walked through the door of their home and dropped his briefcase on the chair.

Saba came running and took a flying leap into his outstretched arms. "Kasi and I were just talking about how fun it would be to visit our friends, Amira and Shatha, but Ummi is busy and we know you won't let us go alone. So, will you take us, please? *Pleeeeeeease!*"

"I'd love to take you girls, but today it's too dangerous."

"What's happened now?" Ummi asked, coming in from the kitchen at the sound of her husband's voice.

"There was so much violence around the school today that we were forced to cancel classes," Dad answered.

"Oh, no! Not again!" Kasi exclaimed.

"Isn't this fighting ever going to stop?" Saba cried. "I'm scared!"

Kasi and Saba's parents were both

teachers in a small town in Iraq. When the war broke out and their safety was threatened, Mom quit teaching to stay home with the girls. It was especially dangerous for their family since they believed in Jesus.

"Girls, Ummi and I need to talk with you about something serious." Kasi and Saba looked at each other with worried looks on their faces.

Dad continued, "It's gotten very dangerous for us here. Our lives have been threatened since we won't give up our faith. As you know, most of the people in our country are Muslims and they don't believe in Jesus. In fact, many of them want to get rid of Christians. I'm afraid of what might happen to our family if the fighting gets much worse."

"Baba, we're not afraid. Jesus will protect us," Kasi replied.

"You're right, Kasi. God can protect us. But I also believe God would like us to make wise decisions. And I don't feel that it is wise to stay here any longer."

"But, Baba, we don't want to leave Amira and Shatha—and all our other friends."

"I understand, but as your father, I need to keep our family safe," Dad said, reaching down and giving his daughters a hug. "Ummi and I have decided to apply for immigration to the United States. Hopefully, we can find good jobs. As you know, Uncle Suhail is a doctor there and his family can help us get settled. Besides, it will be fun for you to get to know your cousins."

At first, the girls cried. They didn't want to leave their friends—or their country for that matter—but when terrorists started bombing their town, they began to pray that God would open a way for them to live in a country where they wouldn't have to be scared.

After months of negotiation, filling out forms, and praying for the doors to open for them to leave their homeland, their visas finally arrived. At last, they were free to leave.

It didn't take Kasi and Saba long to adjust to life in the United States. They soon learned to speak the language. However, even though their parents were teachers, speaking English proved more difficult for them and Kasi and Saba often found themselves translating. Although the girls missed their friends in Iraq, they found America to be new and exciting. What fun they had swimming in the community pool and playing in the neighborhood park with all the fancy playground equipment. They loved the variety of food on the shelves in the grocery stores and the abundance of fresh fruits and vegetables. But mostly, they liked having rooms of their own with air conditioning and going to sleep without worrying about the bombs exploding all around them.

Making friends was more difficult. Since they had come from a Muslim country, which was at war with the United States, many kids treated them as if they were the enemy. Kasi found it particularly challenging. She was more reserved than her younger sister, and her accent was more pronounced than Saba's. It helped that her cousins lived nearby and they had become close friends. In fact, they did everything together.

Then one day her father made an announcement. "Girls, you know that I've been searching for a better job to support our family so that Ummi doesn't have to work so many hours away from home. Well, today I've been offered a new job. It's an excellent opportunity and it pays well too. I will be translating for a large company. The only problem is . . . it will mean moving across country."

"Oh, Baba, you mean we have to leave our cousins?"

"Yes, I'm afraid so," Dad said, nodding his head sympathetically.

looking the other way, so they didn't see him either.

Man, what a ride! Scott's body was still tingling with the adrenaline rush of the exhilarating experience. *I've got to do that again,* he said to himself. He never thought to consider the pool rules. If he had, common sense would have told him that standing up on a slippery slide was forbidden! All he could think about was doing it again!

Just as he got to the top of the slide and stood in his surfing position, his mom caught sight of him and shouted, "Scott! Stop!" but it was too late. He had already pushed off, confident that if he could do it once—he could do it again.

But something went wrong.

Halfway down the slide, he lost his balance, and, instead of diving into the pool when he hit the bottom, he fell backward and CRACK . . . the back of his head hit the end of the slide.

His mom screamed. The lifeguards, who were watching the other children, suddenly looked up as they saw Scott's body drop into the deep end of the pool . . . and disappear.

Friends continued to splash and play, grown-ups continued to talk and laugh, and the hot July sun continued to shine down from a blue summer sky as if nothing unusual had happened. But, under the sparkling surface of the pool, Scott was slowly drifting to the bottom, totally unconscious.

And, like anybody in an unconscious state, his lungs continued to try to breathe, filling them up with heavy, suffocating water.

When Scott failed to surface, his mom yelled, "Help! HELP! My son is drowning!" At the same time, both lifeguards dove into the pool and began to search the bottom. Grabbing Scott's body, they rushed

him to the surface, where Scott immediately went into violent spasms as his oxygen-starved brain tried desperately to find a way to save itself

from certain death. One lifeguard attempted artificial respiration, but Scott's lungs were so filled with water that they wouldn't accept the life-giving air.

"Please save my son!" Scott's mom shouted. She trembled in the arms of another mom as her worst nightmare played out in front of her eyes.

"We've got to get the water out of his lungs," the other lifeguard shouted, grabbing Scott's elbows and stretching his arms above his head. He then folded the boy's knees into his stomach and pressed them firmly.

At first, there was no response. Then Scott let out a terrible groan, followed by a fountain of water that spurted from his mouth and nose. Two more times the lifeguard pressed and two more times water spewed from Scott's body. Finally, air began to enter his lungs.

Slowly, amid a chorus of coughs and sputters, Scott opened his eyes and noticed a ring of frightened people staring down at him. "Do you know where you are?" someone asked.

"At the pool," Scott stammered, unsure of what was going on.

"How many fingers am I holding up?" another queried, thrusting his hand in front of Scott's face, trying to determine if there had been any brain damage.

"Three?" Scott gasped.

Soon, in the distance, the wail of a siren cut through the hot summer air. Scott was put on a stretcher and rushed to the city hospital. His mom sat beside him, holding his hand. "Thank goodness, you're OK," she cried. "That was a bad accident."

"What happened?" Scott asked. "All I remember is losing my balance and falling . . . and then everything went black."

"You were knocked unconscious when you hit your head on the

you're coming with us." Wyatt could tell that his dad's mind was already made up, so he didn't bother arguing. His dad had that look that said the conversation was pretty much over. So, like it or not, bird watching had now taken a prominent spot on his weekend agenda.

Wyatt picked up the bird book that his parents had purchased from the bookstore. He flipped through a few pages. The pictures were colorful. And he realized he had seen many of these birds; he just hadn't always known their names. The sleek gray bird with the black cap looked familiar. Curious, he read its name, *Catbird. No kidding,* he said to himself, *there's a bird named that? It would be fun to find one of those.* He sat down at

the picnic table and continued to read. After learning about their call, he decided that finding a catbird would be a top priority.

"OK, Dad. I'll give it a try." Wyatt laid the book down on the table. Then he smiled at his father, not really wanting to encourage him. *Maybe it won't be that bad,* he thought.

"You're going to have a great time, son. You'll see." His dad grinned back.

Wyatt and his family packed their newly purchased binoculars, bird book, pens, and water bottles in a bag and headed south for a short drive to the trail Aunt Heidi had suggested. Wyatt flipped through the bird book on the way, trying to memorize the names of some of the birds he thought they might see.

"Do you think we'll see the indigo bunting?" his mother asked.

"Aunt Heidi says they're on this trail. But remember, we have to be very quiet and still to get a good look at one." Dad looked into the rearview mirror and smiled at Wyatt. "What color do you think that one is?"

"Let me think . . . indigo?"

"Yeah, but what color is that?"

"Blue."

"Yes, but not just any blue. Wait until we actually see one. From the pictures in the bird book, it's gorgeous. But I'm sure it's even more beautiful in real life."

"Uh-huh." Wyatt nodded and went back to looking at the pictures. He came across the indigo bunting picture and had to admit that it was pretty. He kind of hoped they would see the bright blue bird. He read how it could be found on the edges of the woods, so he knew where he was going to look for one.

Arriving at the trailhead, the family tumbled out of the car, grabbing the different things they needed to begin their first official bird-watching hike.

"This way," Wyatt's dad started out for the trail. He had only gone a few yards when he stopped. *"Shhh."*

"What? What do you see?" Wyatt stopped beside him and looked around.

"Shhh, see that patch of blue?" his father whispered, pointing to some low growing bushes off the side of the main trail.

"Hey, good eyes, Dad. I think it *is* an indigo bunting."

Mom worked at adjusting the binoculars for a closer look. "These things aren't as easy to use as I thought they would be. I'll need some practice."

"Can I try?" Wyatt reached for the binoculars. After a few seconds, he had narrowed in on the bird. He checked the coloring around the beak and saw the black patch. There weren't any wing bars, and the black legs helped confirm his find. "Wow, our first bird!" Wyatt exclaimed. "Don't forget to initial that in the book, Mom, and put our names beside it with the date. Remember how Aunt Heidi told us we could build our list."

Wyatt's parents smiled at each other. Maybe birding would become a family hobby after all.

An hour later, the family had split up, each exploring a different section of the trail to see what they could find. It was a safe family area, so Wyatt was allowed to search for birds on his own.

"Oh, wow!" Wyatt whispered. He turned and made his way back to his parents. "Mom! Dad! Come quick!"

"What did you find?"

"A catbird."

"A what?" Wyatt's mom tipped her head.

"You're making that up, right?" His dad grinned.

"No, really! I found a catbird."

"Pretty funny, son."

"Dad, really. I found a catbird. Come and see." Wyatt turned and headed back down the path. Reluctantly, his parents followed behind.

"*Shhh!* Listen." Wyatt stood perfectly still.

"I hear a kitten."

"No, Mom. That's a catbird." Wyatt pointed across the little creek to a big bush. Perched on the bush was a sleek gray bird with a darker cap. And every time it opened its mouth, the meowing sound of a kitten came out.

"See. It's a catbird." Wyatt opened to the right page and showed his parents.

"Well, I'll be," his dad stammered. "I never knew there was such a thing as a bird making a cat sound."

"Me neither, not until I studied the bird book. Did you know they even mimic the sounds of other birds?" Wyatt's enthusiasm was contagious.

"We've added quite a few birds to our list just today."

"Yes we have, son. We even saw one that I had never heard of before."

"Do you think we can come out here again next weekend, Dad? This is fun."

Wyatt's parents once again smiled at each other. They were glad that Wyatt now understood just how fun birding could be.

"If you think birding is fun here, just think about heaven. How many different kinds of birds will there be? I bet we can spend all eternity just bird watching," commented Dad.

"Yeah," Wyatt agreed, "think how long our birding list will be then!"

Wyatt kept chattering all the way back to the car about how birding was like exploring for treasures that God made. All we have to do is go find them. ■

So God created … every winged bird according to its kind. And God saw that it was good. And God blessed them, saying, … "let birds multiply on the earth." So the evening and the morning were the fifth day.
—Genesis 1:21–23, NKJV

"Deal!" said Cody.

He smiled and grabbed a pen from the table next to his bed and held out his broken arm. "Who wants to be the first to sign my cast?" ■

> *He who covers his sins will not prosper, but whoever confesses and forsakes them will have mercy.*
> —Proverbs 28:13, NKJV

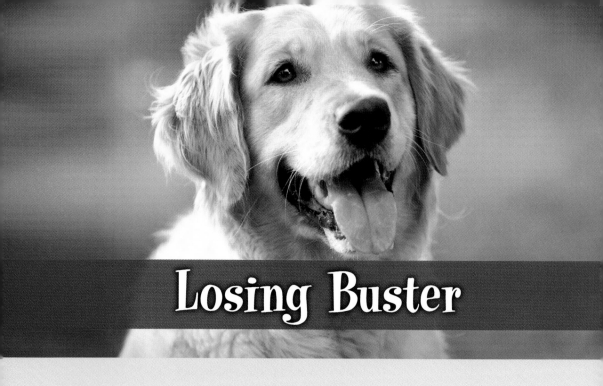

Losing Buster

Jamila burst through the backdoor, wide-eyed and breathless. "Mom! Buster's gone!"

Mom dropped the sheet she was folding back in the laundry basket. "Oh, no!"

Jamila's tears threatened to overflow at any moment. "He dug underneath the side fence and . . ."

Mom raised her eyebrows but didn't say a word.

"I know, I know," said Jamila, "it's my fault. But can we talk about that later? Right now, Buster's gone and we've got to find him!"

"I'll lock the backdoor," said Mom, giving Jamila a squeeze on the way past, "and meet you out front."

Jamila waited impatiently for Mom in front of the mailbox. She had already been up and down the street, calling Buster's name, hoping he had just gone to visit the neighbors, but no such luck. He was gone—really gone!

to break her arm. Her peach tree is loaded. Who is she going to find to pick the peaches that she sells every year to the local market? I think she depends on that money to visit her daughter in Guatemala."

Gabriella immediately called her two friends and exclaimed, "God answered our prayer. We've got our next assignment. Mrs. Gonzales broke her arm. She needs her peaches picked. Let's do it!"

"Great idea!"

When Mrs. Gonzales heard her doorbell ring, she wondered who it could be since it was almost dark. But when she got to the door, no one was there. Then she saw all the baskets of picked peaches on her porch and the note, *Jesus loves you! The Do-Good Club.*

"Well, I declare!" she shouted. "Praise the Lord! I'll call the market manager tomorrow and have him send someone to pick these peaches up. I guess I'll be able to visit my daughter after all."

Next, a single mom with three little children, who was struggling to make ends meet, found a box of groceries next to her apartment door. "What's this?" she questioned. "Is it for me?" She picked up the note. *Dear Mrs. Baxter, Jesus loves you! The Do-Good Club.*

"How did they know our cupboards were almost bare?"

Bridget, Gabriella, and Khloe softly snickered from their hiding place. "I think Jesus let me overhear her little boy say he was hungry when he got off the school bus this morning," Bridget said.

"But what if someone else needs food—or we need to help someone and it takes money? My piggy bank is empty," sighed Khloe.

"Mine too," said Bridget. "I'm going to have to ask the neighbors if they have some odd jobs I can do so I can earn some money."

"Let's pray," Gabriella suggested, "and see if Jesus can help us think of ways we can earn some more money. Helping others is so much fun. I'd hate to not be able to help someone who needs it just because we're all broke!"

After a house burned down in town, the members of the Do-Good Club found out the family had a daughter just their age. So they got together and went through their closets, and with their moms' permission, selected some of the clothes they didn't wear very often to give to the girl. They didn't say who was getting the clothing because even their parents didn't know about the Do-Good Club.

After the box of clothes and other fun things were left on the porch where the family was staying, the newspaper picked up the story. Across the top was the headline, "The Do-Good Club Takes Control of Amesville." The article read, *In the last couple of weeks, it has come to our attention that a new gang is operating in our town. Although most cities are plagued with the crime and violence of gangs fighting for territory and committing criminal acts, there seems to a different type of gang that is making an impact on Amesville. The members call themselves the Do-Good Club, and have distinguished themselves by their random acts of kindness, such as picking peaches for a widow who broke her arm, cleaning off the garage door of elderly Mr. Greer, leaving a box of food for a single mom and her children, and giving clothes to the daughter of the Browns, who lost everything in a fire. Although the identities of the club members are not yet known, they likely will be caught soon as they ring someone's doorbell and run, leaving only a note saying, "Jesus loves you! The Do-Good Club."*

"Oh no!" Bridget groaned. "Did you see that article about the Do-Good Club in the paper?"

"Yeah. Dad mentioned it at breakfast this morning. I was afraid I'd give it away if he looked straight at me and asked if I knew anything about the gang! So I just started coughing and excused myself."

"It's getting more difficult to keep our secret," Gabriella said. "But we can't stop now, especially when they announced at assembly today that Amelia Kemper is sick and won't be able to come back to school. Can you imagine how sad it must be to have to stay in bed all day? We've got to do something to let her know that she's special—and that we care."

"I heard the cancer has spread and she may not have long to live," Bridget added.

"Well then, there's no time to lose. Let's leave her a package everyday so she'll have something to look forward to," suggested Khloe.

On Monday, they delivered some "Hope you're feeling better" notes on handmade cards.

On Tuesday, the girls made some cookies and put them in a basket with some grapes they picked from Bridget's yard.

On Wednesday, they left a puzzle for Amelia to put together.

On Thursday, Amelia's mother was determined to figure out who was leaving the packages for her daughter, so she sat behind the curtain in the living room waiting for the doorbell to ring. Bridget, Gabriella, and Khloe had no idea what was waiting for them at Amelia's house as they dressed up a teddy bear in some doll clothes and wrapped him in a soft baby blanket. "Oh, he's so cute," Bridget squealed.

"Amelia will love him," Khloe said.

"Let's go," Gabriella shouted, "Time to make our *Project Amelia* delivery. I have the *Jesus loves you* card."

Off they rode on their bikes, up Dexter Street and across Avenue B, and then they turned left. They parked their bikes on the opposite side of Amelia's house and were just about to ring the bell when suddenly the front door opened. "Ah, ha! I finally caught the *Do-Good Club*!"

"Oh, Mrs. Kemper, we didn't mean any harm. We just wanted to cheer Amelia up and today we brought her a teddy bear to cuddle while she's in bed," said Bridget as she thrust the bear into Mrs. Kemper's hands.

"Please, don't tell anyone who we are," pleaded Khloe. "We're having so much fun helping others. It just wouldn't be the same if people knew. Please, please, don't say anything!"

"OK, girls. I'll keep your secret—on one condition. That you'll let me be a part of the club. When you need money to fund some good deed, I want you to come to me and let me help you. What do you think? Deal?"

"Wow, Mrs. Kemper, would you really do that for us?" Bridget asked.

"Of course, I would. After what you've done for Amelia—and for the others in town—I'd do anything for you girls. Now quickly run along before someone catches you."

"Thanks," the girls said all at once as they started toward their bikes. Then they stopped, turned around, ran back to Mrs. Kemper, and threw their arms around her. "Welcome to the club!" Bridget said giving her another squeeze.

With a smile on her face, Khloe added, "Be sure to tell Amelia that Jesus loves her and so does the *Do-Good Club*!" ■

> *"Take heed that you do not do your charitable deeds before men, to be seen by them. Otherwise you have no reward from your Father in heaven."*
> —Matthew 6:1, NKJV